A Bit
Muddle

Deborah Shand

Illustrated by Penny Jensz

Momentum
A Bit of A Muddle

First published in Great Britain in 1998 by

Folens Publishers
Albert House
Apex Business Centre
Boscombe Road
Dunstable
Beds LU5 4RL

British Library Cataloguing in Publication Data.
A Catalogue record for this book is available from the British Library

ISBN 1 86202 418 9

Designed by Tom Kurema
Printed in Singapore by PH Productions Pte Ltd

I don't mean to cause trouble; it's just that things sometimes get in a bit of a muddle. What happened last Tuesday really wasn't my fault. I knew that I had swimming lessons after school, but Dad must have forgotten. I'm sure I gave him the note.

Anyway, I took my swimming gear to school on Tuesday and went down to the pool right after class. I didn't know that Monica, our sitter, was waiting for me at the school gate with Abby, my little sister. Monica picks us up from school and takes us home every day.

After waiting for a while, Monica went to see my teacher to see if I'd been kept after school. When she found out I hadn't been, she went to see the headteacher. She phoned my father from the headteacher's office.

About then, I would have been swimming the backstroke.

Dad was in a meeting when Monica phoned and told him I was missing. "Maybe he didn't see you and went around to his grandparents' house," Dad suggested. Their house is about a ten-minute walk from my school.

So, while I was swimming freestyle, Monica and Abby drove around to my grandparents' house. Grandma was playing croquet, and Grandpa was teaching their old dog, Frump, new tricks. They stopped what they were doing when they saw Monica and Abby.

“No, Harvey’s not here,” said Grandma.

“We wouldn’t have any biscuits left if he was,” agreed Grandpa.

“Maybe he decided to walk home,” suggested Grandma.

“I’ll drive around there and see,” said Grandpa.

“I’ll stay here and phone his friends,” said Grandma.

“I’ll drive around the streets and look for him,” said Monica.

“I’ll play croquet,” said Abby.

“Everyone meet back here in 15 minutes,” said Grandma. “If we haven’t found Harvey by then, we’ll call the police.”

About that time, I was just starting on my breaststroke.

Suddenly my father jumped up in the middle of his meeting and shouted, "That's where he'll be!" He rushed out to call the headteacher. He had remembered that I was at my swimming lesson.

But the headteacher had gone home. So Dad tried to get hold of Harry Nutwell, but he was scrubbing the school's floors and didn't hear the phone. So Dad tried my grandparents' number, but the line was busy because Grandma was calling my friends' parents.

And I was climbing out of the pool because my swimming lesson was over.

When Grandpa got to our house, he found the back door open. In the morning rush, one of us must have forgotten to shut it. In my room, drawers were pulled out and things were all over the floor. This is normal for me, but Grandpa thought that burglars had been there. There was no sign of me.

He tried to phone Grandma, but her line was still busy. Then he tried Dad, but his phone was busy because he was trying to call Grandma. So Grandpa thought he'd better not waste any more time. He phoned the police to report a possible kidnapping.

Meanwhile, Monica was driving around looking for me. But she forgot to watch her fuel gauge. As she was driving down the street, the car stopped and wouldn't start again. So she set off on foot to look for a phone to get help.

By this time I was dry and dressed. I headed up to the school gate, thinking Monica and Abby would be there to meet me. On the way, I noticed Harry Nutwell down on his knees in a doorway. At first I thought he was inspecting for termites, but then I saw that he was hanging on to the door. He was making an awful noise in his throat.

"Help," he gasped.

I ran over to him, but he slid down to the floor and wheezed, "Doctor, doctor." So I dropped my bag and sprinted back to the pool to get help.

Grandma was worried. Twenty minutes had passed since Grandpa and Monica had left, and they had not returned yet. Grandma tried to call Grandpa at our house, but there was no answer because Grandpa was out in the street talking to the police. So Grandma called Dad.

"At last!" said Dad. "I've been trying to get you. I think Harvey has gone to swimming lessons. Get Monica or Grandpa to check the pool."

"I can't do that," Grandma said. "I seem to have lost Monica and Grandpa! But Abby and I will walk over and check the pool ourselves."

"I'll meet you at the school," said Dad. "It's time for me to finish work anyway."

So Grandma scribbled a note for Monica and Grandpa in case they returned. It said: 'Gone to School, suspect Swimming.' She taped it to the front door, and set off with Abby and Frump.

I raced down to the pool. "Quick!" I shouted to the swimming coach. "Harry Nutwell needs a doctor! He sounds as if he's been strangled!"

The coach picked up the phone. "Quick!" he said. "Send an ambulance and the police. A man has been strangled!" He gave the address of the school, and then he followed me down the hall.

"Asthma," Harry wheezed.

"It's okay, Harry," said the coach. "The ambulance will be here soon."

COACH

Monica was still trying to find a phone when she saw a police car with its siren wailing and its lights flashing. It screeched to a stop in front of her. A policeman and a policewoman were in the front. Grandpa was in the back.

"Hop in!" Grandpa called. "We think Harvey's been kidnapped!"

They tore off to Grandma and Grandpa's house, where they found Grandma's note.

"Suspect swimming!" exclaimed the policeman. "What is the suspect doing swimming? This sounds fishy to me!"

As they got back into the police car, a message came crackling over the radio. "Calling car 17! Investigate strangling at local school."

"This sounds serious!" said the policewoman. "Someone has burgled a house and kidnapped a child, been swimming and strangled someone. We'd better not waste any time!"

They didn't see Grandma and Abby taking a shortcut through the park, and the police car arrived at the school first. I was just running up to the gate as it pulled up. Monica and Grandpa jumped out and hugged me. "You're safe!" they cried.

"Of course," I said calmly. "What did you expect?"

The policewoman stuck her head out of the car window and growled, “Where is he?”

Thinking they had come to help Harry Nutwell, I pointed to the door. “Inside,” I said.

The police ran inside as an ambulance came screaming around the corner. It screeched to a stop and the ambulance attendants raced after the police.

“Wait,” I said to Monica and Grandpa. “I’ve left my schoolbag inside!” I ran inside after the ambulance attendants.

“Wait!” called Grandpa and Monica, and they ran after me.

The swimming coach was crouching over Harry Nutwell. "You're under arrest!" called the policeman. "Raise your hands!"

The bewildered coach put his hands in the air.

The ambulance attendants trotted over to Harry Nutwell with a stretcher.

"We'll soon have you out of here," they said, and put an oxygen mask over his nose and mouth. Harry's face was turning blue. Outside, the ambulance attendants loaded Harry into the ambulance. The police handcuffed the coach and were ready to take him away.

As Grandma and Abby came walking up with Frump, my dad's car roared around the corner and screeched to a stop. He ran into everyone at the door!

"Ah, good, I've found you all," said Dad, smiling. "But, what's going on here?"

"I think things have got in a bit of a muddle," I answered.